EARLY PRAISE FOR *TO LOSE THE MADNESS*

"Browning brings us inside the disoriented unfolding of a life taking new shape after trauma. This is not a 'tie a neat bow around it' trauma and recovery story with a too-simple happy ending, but a messy, honest look at a life that will never be the same."

   –LILLY DANCYGER, Deputy Editor of *Narratively*

"*To Lose the Madness* is an essay built from the bones of the earth. Browning offers a stripped down, belly-to-the-ground, howling manifesto to authenticity, the truth that resides beneath layers of flesh and soil. It is a roadmap of hard-won scars and suffering, the kind of suffering that carves a life like glaciers carve landscapes. Where it has been, a riverbed of beauty and self-knowledge has been left."

   –JASON KIRKEY, author of *The Salmon in the Spring*

"This is Browning's most personally revealing book to date—and perhaps her best. It is a book that offers a brief but deep glimpse at a writer's soul, and, in doing so, a glimpse at our own."

   –THEODORE RICHARDS, author of *Cosmosophia*

"*To Lose the Madness* is poignant, it is granular and gritty, it sings. From the depth of a despair often not spoken for, Browning offers her reader a compassionate voice of witnessing for herself and for anyone who has been touched by this kind of suffering."

   –GARY W

To Lose the Madness

To Lose the Madness

Field Notes on Trauma, Loss and Radical Authenticity

PHOTOS AND ESSAY BY

———

L.M. BROWNING

THE LITTLE BOUND BOOKS ESSAY SERIES

Personal. Poignant. Powerful.

The author has tried to recreate events, locales and conversations from
her memories of them. In order to maintain their anonymity in some
instances she has changed the names of individuals and places, she may
have changed some identifying characteristics and details such as physical
properties, occupations and places of residence.

Published in 2018 • Little Bound Books
Imprint of Homebound Publications
Front Cover Image © Lauren Mancke (Flickr)
Interior Photography © Leslie M. Browning
Cover and Interior Designed • Leslie M. Browning
Author Photo © "Mallory"
*While the author would have liked to have included her own image for the
cover, she was experiencing the moment and therefore had no means of
documentation; however, the photos on the interior of the book are by the
author and follow the course of the trip West.*

ISBN • 978-1-947003-90-3 • First Edition Trade Paperback

Library of Congress Cataloging-in-Publication Data

Names: Browning, L. M., author. Title: To lose the madness : field notes
on trauma, loss and radical authenticity / by L.M. Browning.
Description: First edition. | Pawcatuck, CT : Little Bound Books, 2018.
| Includes bibliographical references. Identifiers: LCCN 2017055727 |
ISBN 9781947003903 (trade paperback) Subjects: LCSH: Browning, L.
M.--Mental health. | Post-traumatic stress disorder–Patients–Biography.
Classification: LCC RC552.P67 B77 2018 | DDC 616.85/210092 [B] –
DC23LC record available at https://lccn.loc.gov/2017055727

10 9 8 7 6 5 4 3 2 1

Homebound Publications is committed to ecological stewardship.
We greatly value the natural environment and invest in environmental
conservation. Our books are printed on paper with chain of custody
certification from the Forest Stewardship Council, Sustainable Forestry
Initiative, and the Program for the Endorsement of Forest Certification.

New Mexico

"The world that used to nurse us
now keeps shouting inane instructions.
That's why I ran to the woods."
—JIM HARRISON, *Songs of Unreason*

Cimarron Valley, New Mexico

———

THE STARK GOLDEN PRAIRIE STRETCHED out to the base of the eastern slopes of the Sangre de Cristo Mountains. Among the overgrown grasses, dry wooden fences rose. The posts were strung together by braided barbed wire that carried from one pole to the next. Just beyond the wire, we saw them—hulking, horned, billowing heavy breaths through their wide nostrils into the chilled December air.

It was the day after Christmas. We traveled down U.S. Route 64, en route to Taos. We were just outside of Cimarron Valley in northern New Mexico when they came into sight. "Buffalo!" exclaimed Mallory and I simultaneously in the otherwise quiet car. A herd of brown, thick-coated bison flew by the drivers-side window. Mallory quickly pulled a U-turn on the deserted country road. We got out of the car and slowly approached them.

In the language of the Lakhóta, the name for the buffalo is *thathánka*. The buffalo was held in sacred regard by the tribe. The great animal gave everything it had to the people—its flesh for food, its hide for shelter and clothing, its bone and sinew for everything from needles to tools. The buffalo stands as a symbol of self-sacrifice—it gives until there is nothing left—and in doing so makes life possible for the people.[1]

As I stood there—my creased leather boots breaking through the stiff, frosty grass—I looked dark eye to dark eye—a single female buffalo moved out of the herd and began walking toward me. I was reminded of a painting I saw as a child by Robert Bateman of a buffalo emerging from behind a veil of thick mist. I was transfixed. Here I was broken—a shadow of myself—and she a wild thing, untamed, and strength untold. Some otherworldly grace encircled us. In the space between us, we spoke of the ineffable things—of what it is to sacrifice all of one's self, of grief, and gratitude—and of the terms every living thing must come to.

Cimarron Valley, New Mexico

BEYOND THE LIMIT

"All living things contain a measure of madness that
moves them in strange, sometimes inexplicable ways.
This madness can be saving; it is part and parcel of the
ability to adapt. Without it, no species would survive."
— YANN MARTEL, *Life of Pi*

One Year Earlier

THERE WAS A HEAVY SURGE OF BLOOD and clear fluid streaking down my leg and onto the dusty bathroom floor. My heart fell hard and fast into my stomach. A full breath of terror caught in my chest. For a fleeting moment, I thought it was the cyst finally rupturing; having had been diagnosed with an advanced case of endometriosis a few years previous. "There is a cyst," I can still remember the specialist explaining, "right in the shared-wall between your uterus and intestine." He concluded darkly as he peeled back the purple latex glove he wore while I sat on the hard examining table—two stirrups jetting out in front of me. I still wrapped in a sheer paper drape from the waist down. The nurse placed the aggressive transvaginal ultrasound wand thickly coated in KY jelly upright in its holster. While a frozen black and white etching of my shadowy cervix flickered on the screen.

"What happens now?" I asked, dumbstruck and disoriented.

"Well, we will discuss treatment options but really it is a wait-and-see scenario."

"Wait and see if what...?" I asked.

"Wait and see if—or when—the cyst will require surgical intervention. The surgery is extremely unpleasant so let's hope it doesn't come to that." He finished before shooting me an encouraging smile and exiting the room.

More blood surged down my leg. My heart raced as I rushed for a washcloth. Fiber and sinew followed, the form of which helped me to realize exactly what was happening. No, it wasn't the cyst. It was my other greatest fear come to pass—the reality of which I couldn't even bear to face. Panicking, grief-stricken, terrified, a swell of overwhelming emotion amalgamated into a wall of solid denial the depths of which I never had before experienced in my life.

After spending a suspiciously-long period of time in the bathroom, I emerged weak-legged and shaken into the living room where I laid myself upon the sofa.

"Are you alright?" Noah asked. A look of concern creased his face.

"I'm fine." I quickly answered. "Just passed some tissue," I added, trying to convince myself as much as him. It wasn't an altogether odd occurrence for me to pass endometrial tissue given the advanced stage of my disease. "I think my period is starting." I reinforced.

Of course, it wasn't my monthly cycle. I just *needed* it to be. I turned towards the T.v.—gaze firmly fixed. I still felt Noah's eyes staring at me but I couldn't meet them. I had to focus on the T.v.. I stared at the still-frame of a cooking show we'd been watching, paused mid-sentence since I went into the bathroom a lifetime ago. I needed to focus on something trivial. The last two years had been unbearable. I couldn't endure anything else, let alone this.

The health issues had begun a few years back. I'd been subjected to a gauntlet of invasive procedures, a major abdominal surgery, and a traumatizing number of ultrasounds and pelvic exams that went above and beyond the normal. Then, on the very first day I attempted to rebuild my strength and stamina from these procedures, I suffered a horrible fall that left me with a *Trimalleolar* fracture of my left leg and dislocated ankle, which resulted in what is termed an "unstable fracture" that could only be mended through surgical intervention. I'd spend the next year after the surgery learning how to walk again.

Running concurrently with this assault of medical testing and the extensive injury was a string of unprecedented bad luck including numerous bouts with pneumonia, a car accident that resulted in a neck injury, and other challenges I won't go into. Needless to say, I was never in such ragged shape. After everything my body had been through, I was facing a psychological backlash as well. The intimate nature of many of the procedures I was put through to pinpoint the Endometriosis left me in an emotionally fragile state. I'd suffered too much too fast.

The Palisades, Cimarron Canyon, New Mexico

THE END OF DENIAL

"Out beyond ideas of wrongdoing and rightdoing,
there is a field. I'll meet you there."
—JALALUDDIN RUMI

"I MISCARRIED TWINS BACK IN AUGUST," I confessed to Mallory from across the table. We were tucked away in a local bar, done with dinner and well into cocktails. It was the first time I'd allowed myself to *think it,* let alone *speak it,* since that afternoon in the bathroom over two months back. A vodka-fueled confession brought me face-to-face with the subconscious thought that had been causing me to unravel further and further down my psyche for the intervening 8 weeks.

The denial I experienced was as dense as the darkest night. I had not yet gone to the doctor. I still hadn't told Noah what had happened. We had been through hardships that had tested our emotional connection over our relationship and we'd come to learn we each handled these hard times in our own—very opposite—way. If I told him, I knew we'd both be isolated: me in my pain, which needed to be expressed and addressed, and him in the silence he needed to cope with the harshness life brings.

With this latest blow, my mind had been brought to the limit of what could be borne and, driven to keep the organism moving forward, my mind pushed away a reality that I couldn't face and I entered denial. Something about Mallory though invited an emergence from that denial; however, immediately after I said the word "miscarriage" the reality my mind had avoided impaled me.

We walked back to my office around the corner from the bar and there we stayed until dawn. I'd just signed the lease. The room was small, quiet, and bare. That night, I came into the frame of mind where I couldn't bear this life another day, and while it scares me to dwell on it, I can honestly say, I don't know what would have happened had Mallory not been there.

That night, I laid curled up on the floor hysterical, suspended in grief, sleep deprived, and wholly undone. I had to accept everything lost, everything said, and everything yet-to-be-faced-but-swiftly-coming. The miscarriage had been the mental last straw. I couldn't hold myself together, but thankfully, she held me together as the hours drew out.

In the coming weeks, Noah and I would part ways, ending our 8-year relationship. Truth be told, the relationship had ended years before, neither of us simply had the heart to walk away from one another. We had spent years talking to one another about everything except what we really needed to discuss, not because we were indifferent to those issues creating distance between us but because we knew there was no resolution to be had, only a parting, and the reality of that was too sad to face.

All I knew was, we'd done everything we could to make it work—we'd emptied ourselves upon the altar of our relationship only to remain empty—and, at the close, we simply wanted one another to be happy, even if it meant parting ways.

Cimarron, New Mexico

COMING APART

"I had nothing to offer anybody except
my own confusion." –JACK KEROUAC

FOLLOWING THESE EVENTS, I was left horribly fractured. I had reached a point where I could no longer function in my life. I entered therapy in an effort to "process" what had happened, not only in recent years but over the years before, which were no easier, and learn how to "let go." I was in what my therapist termed a "severe depressive episode" and was suicidal. I was in therapy for only 6 or 8 weeks to "stabilize" when the deeper diagnoses came of Complex Post Traumatic Stress Syndrome (C-PTSD) and Mild Dissociative Disorder. I was referred to a trauma specialist to begin intensive therapy and a treatment called E.M.D.R..

The C-PTSD didn't come about as a result of the miscarriage or successions of injuries alone. It was a combination of being raised in the company of malignant narcissists who held direct sway over my sense of self, living with abusive drunks who terrorized me as a small child, and having been the victim of one blind-siding incident after another. The miscarriage and injuries in the years that preceded the breakdown simply brought the full weight of the pain to bear.

In her book, *Trauma and Recovery,* Judith Lewis Herman explains the roots of C-PTSD (the lesser-known cousin to PTSD,): "Situations causing the kind of traumatic stress that can lead to C-PTSD include captivity or entrapment . . . as well as psychological manipulation, which can result in a prolonged sense of helplessness and deformation of one's identity and sense of self." Those individuals who suffer from C-PTSD have experienced long-term exposure to emotional trauma over which, "a victim has little or no control and from which there is little or no hope of escape, such as in cases of: domestic abuse, repeated violations of personal boundaries . . . or long-term exposure to crisis conditions."[2]

Stuck within the dark thoughts and simply wanting to heal, I went to the trauma specialist as instructed and began a therapy to treat the C-PTSD known as E.M.D.R. In principle, Eye Movement Desensitization and Reprocessing (E.M.D.R.) is a psychotherapy that enables victims of trauma to heal from wounds that have been inflicted as a result of disturbing life experiences. In a 8-part therapy, a patient processes a trauma and, unlike talk therapy, which can take years, E.M.D.R. helps the individual to process the trauma within a matter of days or weeks. The therapy, in theory, enables the victim to process the emotions at the root of the trauma without being triggered by recalling the incidences that brought about the distress.

In my experience, which I've been told is an exceptionally poor one, E.M.D.R. is like someone entering the darkest—most buried—part of your mind, awakening all the hungry ghosts and leaving you with them. Unbeknownst to me at the time, my clinician didn't follow the full protocol for the treatment. I didn't get the 8-part therapy but a scattershot blast to the psyche, which left me fragmented and bleeding. The clinician in question hopped from trauma to trauma with no stabilization process and little pre-procedure assessment. All of which resulted in extreme "emotional flooding" and destabilization.

A few weeks into the E.M.D.R., I began having "episodes." In the episodes, I'd cycle from being triggered, to full-tilt rage, to fight or flight, to the crash into the bleakest despair, to exhaustion, and back again. Each episode lasted upwards of 5 hours and reoccurred on a bi-weekly basis. This cycle was unbearable to both myself and those around me.

The miscarriage had emotionally leveled me but this process was a mental dismemberment from which it seemed there would be no recovery.

I told the specialist about the episodes and she said, "Stay with it. It will get worse before it gets better. You will be able to let go of what happened to you and heal." Determined as I was to heal, I kept going and the episodes only increased in frequency. Finally, almost four months after starting the therapy, I felt no choice but to suspend the sessions. It wasn't until later, when I confided in a colleague who was once a therapist of my experience, that I found out that my "specialist" hardly lived up to her job title and that her work had essentially induced another trauma all its own.

The episodes continued to occur weekly for another ten months; as though slipping into that state became the default position for my brain when handling stress. Over these dark months, I came to see quite easily how someone with mental illness can become homeless. As ill as you are, you can't work and yet, given that mental illness still struggles to be regarded as a true "illness" and not a personal failing, it is hard to get financial support or medical leave to see one's self through such periods. Then, the small support system one who is ill has—while loving and loyal—have their limits and when they feel as though they have done all that they can and still the illness rages, they feel hopeless and change from a mindset of helping you to protecting their own well-being. Finally, the one who is ill feels like a burden to those closest to them (who often take the brunt of the rage and sadness from the one who suffers from PTSD struggles with), so much so that they can choose to go off on their own if only to spare their loved ones the damaging proximity to a pain that is beyond control. While I, thankfully, didn't end up homeless, I can clearly see how such a fall from functioning to destitution takes place.

Colorado Springs, Colorado

THERE IS NO LETTING GO

———————

"As my sufferings mounted I soon realized that there
were two ways in which I could respond to
my situation—either to react with bitterness
or seek to transform the suffering into a creative force.
I decided to follow the latter course."

—MARTIN LUTHER KING JR.

THERE IS NO "LETTING GO." I would dare to take it further and say there is no healing from trauma. For nearly 25 years, I've waited to *get over* the traumas that have amassed across my life. The pursuit of this healing has felt a great deal like a search for God—for something elusive, divine, and that may or may not exist.

To say I woke up one day and reached a point where I no longer cared about the pains to befall me would be a lie. Nor can I say that I have ever fully forgiven those who willfully did me harm. On a deep, internal battlefield, I wrestle with the thought that I have been robbed of any chance of normalcy by the losses suffered. Therapists and gurus alike tell us to, "Let go or be dragged," as Zen proverb urges—to forgive for our own sake. But, in my experience, there is no letting go and forgiveness is transient. My inability to be free of it all isn't for lack of an evolved consciousness on my part. I've "done the work" to process it all; rather, it is my irreconcilable, inescapable humanity that causes to clutch the pain close to me.

In lieu of letting go of our trauma and rather than healing completely, in my experience, we learn how to carry it and there are some days when it is heavier than others. Some days, I hardly know it is there, distracted as I am by present joys and excitement; while other days, the burden is cripplingly-heavy and I can hardly breathe under the weight of grief.

In the terms of my miscarriage, knowing that there is no letting go means I will carry my children with me. I will grieve for the life not lived, what Cheryl Strayed calls "the sister life." In her advice column, *Dear Sugar,* she writes, "I'll never know and neither will you, of the life you don't choose. We'll only know that whatever that sister life was, it was important and beautiful and not ours. It was the ghost ship that didn't carry us. There's nothing to do but salute it from the shore." For myself, I would have chosen that life but it didn't choose me. It didn't carry me but I will carry it.

In the months following the miscarriage, I broke down one day. I was at home with my mother. She tried to console me as I asked, "I wonder when I will stop counting."

Her look begged an explanation. I went on, "Every so often, I find myself counting how old the twins would be had they been born."

She nodded sympathetically.

"You won't ever stop counting," she answered gently and knowingly.

It was then and there that I knew I would never "let go" or "get over" what had happened and striving to do so was the purist of some form of repression and repression is what had led to the breakdown and even more grief. We can't deny our journey. We can't pretend we're fine when we're not. All we can do is *own it*—own our suffering.

Before the breakdown, I used to hide the unsavory struggles of my past—flatten myself out socially so that I wouldn't be so different that others would find me hard to understand and therefore embrace. I tried to make the messy, neat; the odd, normal; and the complex, simple. But in doing so I portrayed myself as a watered-down version of who I am and eventually lost my truth among the white lies.

Now I know, you can't change what's happened to you, or hide it, or spin it, or get over it. All you can do is hold it confidently knowing that the mistakes are yours but so too is the wisdom earned along the punishing passage. Suffering is the catalyst for transformation. The wounds don't define us; how we went about surviving does. Oddity, in this sickened society of medicated despair, is a blessed state.

As I write this now, the twins would be turning one-year-old. I hold this perpetually turning number within me just as I hold all the firsts that will never come to pass. It is the weight of what shall never come to be that must be carried. In the beginning—right after it happened—the weight was too much. All that *they* would have been, all that *I* would have been, all that *we* would have been—the weight of it was suffocating.

Eagle's Nest, New Mexico

THE NEXT HORIZON

———————

"The mountains are calling and I must go."
—JOHN MUIR

So broken, so lost, so tired, so innocent and yet so guilty, I was forlorn in this world and coming apart at every seam. Yet, there was one solace during this time—a new friendship—found in Mallory. It was somehow healing to be at Mal's side. To know that she could see me, she understood what she saw, and cared enough to tend to me and hold me together hour after hour when every part of me came unraveled was tremendous. It was the most precious gift one soul can give to another. She was at once my doctor, my friend, my sanctuary, and an integral thread within my braided tether mooring me to this earth during a time when I was disconnected from myself and my sanity.

While I had spoken of the miscarriage and went on to have the subsequent breakdown when the denial was breached, some part of me remained disconnected. Most days, I reassured my mind and heart that the events in the bathroom that day had indeed been a cyst rupturing and not a miscarriage. Of course, the doctor reports contradicted that comforting fiction. In the weeks following my confession, Mallory had taken me to the doctor's office where the loss was confirmed. But, even with the confirmation, I was still running away. I remember wandering through stores only to come to the baby department and pull back tears. I avoided eye contact with small children in stores and made wide circles to dodge playgrounds wherever possible.

I can still remember the first time when, instead of saying, "I'm sorry you had to go through *that* [the miscarriage]" someone said to me, "I'm sorry you had to lose *them*." My eyes closed tight and my mind recoiled at the *them*. I had admitted to the miscarriage—to the medical event—but had in no way faced the full extent of what had been lost. I pushed the idea of the twins from my mind with vehement force, not because I didn't care but because I cared too much to bear it.

Wrung out after the weekly grind of the episodes, Mallory came to me one freakishly warm day in late November as I sat out on the deck of her apartment watching the Connecticut River flow. "We both have 10 days off over Christmas. I think we should drive west to Arizona. I haven't been back to Sedona in years."

"You want to drive to Arizona?" I looked up from my thoughts, my eyes shadowed from lack of sleep. "That's like 2500 miles, one-way. It will take days."

"You've never been West and you keep saying you want to see the mountains. Neither of us ever get time off." She reasoned. Her dark brown eyes fixed on me. I still looked hesitant.

"We're writers. We need new experiences," she added.

How could I argue with that?

And so it was that I came to be along the side of Route 64 outside of the Sangre de Cristo Mountains on the day after Christmas.

Sangre de Cristo is Spanish for "Blood of Christ." This namesake is rumored to be rooted in the burnt red coloring the rising and setting sun casts upon the otherwise-white snow. "Sangre de Cristo" is, of course, the latest term for a range that has gone by many names throughout history, be it in Native American, Spanish, or English. A few of the other names the mountains have gone by are *La Sierra Madre* and simply "The Snowies."[3] The range is the southernmost branch of the Rocky Mountains.

Throughout the journey West, I had a raging fever. In a mere two days, we drove 1,925 miles from Connecticut to Colorado Springs, where we chose to break our journey. The further West we went, the sicker I seemed to become. As though the turmoil, rage, and grief within me were tightening their coiled grip, sensing that something was coming that would force it to relinquish their hold.

We would enter Colorado Springs by night on Christmas Day. We were a few hours out when, driving along the back roads into the city, Mal suddenly pulled over along the shoulder of the barren road we were on.

"What are you doing?" I turned to her from the passenger seat.

"Get out of the car." She urged as she opened her door. The frigid wind caught the door as she opened it and she had to fight to close it again.

"It's freezing." I shivered through chattering teeth, slamming my door shut.

"Just look up." She instructed gently.

I turned my gaze upward and stared into the dense darkness—squinting through the cutting wind—and there, in the clarity above, at 6,000 ft above sea level, without the pollution of the city lights, lay bare the Milky Way. Threads of blue and gold flowed into clouds of cream and violet, with a spray of stars running like a river above us. In that moment of awe, I couldn't feel the bite of the wind or the fatigue of the fever; the dome of the night sky engulfed me. My world was turned upside-down and I fell into this womb of light, color, and calm.

We drove on. By the time we hit Colorado Springs around 11 p.m., the fever was high—inducing blurred vision and the sweats. After a quick snack from the only bar in town open on holiday, we found a cheap motel and crashed hard.

When we had arrived, the surrounding range—Pike's Peak, at 14,114 ft, being the tallest—were obscured by the cloud cover shrouding the moon's light. Come morning, it was time to see the new horizon. In the weeks before the miscarriage, I'd lined up a trip to Glacier National Park in Montana because, for years, there had been in me a growing hunger to see the mountains—snowy capped and graceful. After the years spent isolated in recovery from the various ailments, I longed to be engulfed by the wild silence—I wanted to recapture the ability to be still and be brought to a moment of awe and grace. Sadly, the trip was canceled in light of the events. Mallory knew the pull the West had over me. She was a seasoned traveler having made dozens of cross-country treks between her homes in Arizona and Connecticut.

When at last the morning came, Mallory and I climbed into the car to begin the search for a café for breakfast. Mal drove out—beyond the tall buildings—and the imposing monument of Pike's Peak finally came into view. I hid my face from her—staring directly out the passenger window at the snow spinning off the summits—eyes welling up with tears. Some part of me thought I'd never get a chance to see this site—never get beyond Connecticut, beyond illness, beyond financial circumstance, beyond the vacuum of the trauma—yet there they were, on the edge of my new horizon.

We lingered for a time gazing at the mountains before going to breakfast. After a hearty meal, which thankfully came on a plate, contained green vegetables and had never passed through a microwave, we set out for the outskirts of the city and the red rock formations of the Garden of the Gods.

It is said that numerous native tribes had a relationship with the Garden of the Gods, including Apache, Cheyenne, Comanche, Lakhóta, Pawnee, and Ute to name a few. The spires and waves of sandstone and limestone tell tales of long-forgotten seas and eroded mountain ranges.[4] A surreal movement is there in the field of stone monuments even though they are motionless.

I am a New Englander through and through. Mallory once put it best when she said my heart was made of flannel and cider. She, by contrast, is a woman of the Southwest. As we drove, she told me of the landscape she was bringing me to and how differently it moved as compared to the Northeast. She reflected that the Northeast is tightly packed— claustrophobic almost—the horizon is closer and you mistakenly start to feel big but, when you drive across the country and come out here—out West— everything is bigger; the horizon is wider and you can see just how small you are in the grander scheme of things. There is a magic here that can help the mind breathe.

*　　*　　*　　*

Pulling ourselves away, we drove the U.S. 24 and over to U.S. 64 down to Taos, along the old Santa Fe Trail. It was there that we encountered the Buffalo, and this account began.

Leaving the graceful beasts behind, we moved into Cimarron Canyon. The winding roads were iced over; falling rocks and high winds revealed our ill-equipped Toyota sedan to be a comical choice of rental car. We crept along slow and steady, which not only kept us alive over the treacherous terrain but gave us a chance to take in our surroundings. The trees loomed tall outside the window. Stacked squares of boulder seemed to piece together the greater mountain; all leading to Palisades—a 400-foot sheer granite outcrop within the canyon. Aspen groves followed the banks of the Cimarron River; while towering Fir trees blanketed the south side of the canyon.

We pressed on through Cimarron to the town of Eagle's Nest, where the road turns south towards Taos, through the Carson National Forest where the red earth bled into the white snow along the roadside.

Mal decided we would break our journey in Taos at the house of some old friends of hers. As disaffected as I was, I was hesitant to stay with strangers but she asked me to trust her. She pointed out that she never surrounds herself with toxic people and that Mark and Sara were good hearts.

Mark and Sara's house was an old adobe structure, one level. Walking in, I took in the warmth of our hosts and surrogate home. The straw was still visible in the mud walls. There were exposed wood beams and red tile floor with a single wood stove that heated the whole house. A small, endearing Christmas tree was cozily tucked in a corner. One of the two dogs, Hawk, a two-year-old husky-pit mix, followed me around. He had white-blue eyes and emotionally reflective ears; he reminded me of a wolf and harkened to that small girl in me that loved reading *White Fang* and who so desperately wanted to live in Alaska when she grew up.

I was to sleep in Mark's music room during our stay—an 8 x 8 room that he tells us was the original building—Mark, like Mallory, was a singer-songwriter; the room held an upright bass and an assortment of Guild guitars. I walked the edges of the small room. The mud walls crumble a bit more in this room than the others. Books and old cameras lined the back wall of the room where my bed was laid out. Sara had impeccably decorated the house; it was authentic New Mexico without being tacky or overstated; there was all-encompassing authenticity to both them and the home they'd created.

Before turning in for the night, I stumbled feverishly and wearily into the shower. After 34 hours in the car, 2 uncomfortably unclean hotel rooms and an obscene diet of takeout, the idea of being in a home with kind, welcoming people, a spacious shower, and a crisp bed of clean sheets with a heavy Woolrich blanket laid out on it bound like a bandage around my vagabond soul. I'd been living out of a bag since the miscarriage—evicted by the hand of circumstance from the life I'd had and still trying to find the place where I now belonged.

That night, as the warm water beat heavily upon me, I felt the blood and tears and weariness flow off me. There was something honest about Mark and Sara's house—the fire in the stove, the simplicity, the truthfulness of their way of life. Both of them had lived and worked in New York for a number of years—in the very epicenter of hustle, bustle, and ego—only to move out to live on a sparse hill in Taos, at the base of the mountains alone because it was the place that called to their heart.

After scrubbing the weariness from my bones I crawled into bed and stared up into the dark stillness and it came.... Everything that had collected within me rained down and I slipped beneath the wave of memories never made but somehow held nonetheless. The images came fast like a reel of two lives playing out in my mind—the birth, each of them being laid down upon my chest, the night bottles, the first steps, the first days of school, birthday parties, books read aloud in bed, holidays around the Christmas tree, teenage heartbreaks, rebellious fights and mended fences, college acceptance letters, the weddings and finally the grandchildren being placed in my arms.

The images, having run their course, stopped and I was left lying there in the silence. I'd run from their death and, in doing so, run from their life then gone mad somewhere in the dark distance in-between the two. I cried the entire night—deep sobs. At last, I had them. They were mine, safe and sound. My mind, so taut and tormented, released.

Emerging from the fever into mourning, I carry the faces of my children clearly in my mind. I alone know their names. Within me they have lived a full life—within me we became all that we would have been.

No sleep came that night but oddly I woke rested. The next morning, as I sat there on the sofa, a warm ceramic mug of coffee in my hand, my journal open on my lap, Hawk sitting next to me—his wild, ice-blue eyes looking deep into me—while Mallory and Mark strummed on their guitars and their voices traveled in-between the warm acoustics of the wood beams and adobe walls, the snowy slopes of the Sangre de Cristo Mountains were framed perfectly in the bay window. In that moment, I knew something was starting after years of things ending. Loss no longer dominated my thoughts. Hope, however faint, had subtly entered. I knew that, despite all that had come to pass, there were still good days left to me and new horizons to behold.

*   *   *   *

In the film adaptation of Jim Harrison's novella, *Legends of the Fall*, we follow the story of the war-wearied character Colonel Ludlow who, after watching the butchering of the Native Americans, gives up his post. To "lose the madness over the mountains and begin again", he sets off and moves to the remote frontier of Montana where he hopes to raise his three sons in a more-just world of his own creation. The character of the disillusioned warrior soothed by the simplicity and silence of nature is an archetype of this war-driven, industrialized era. It is the story arc that traces the trail of the once-idealistic-now-misanthropic protagonist led astray by progressing culture who ultimately finds themselves and a long-sought truce with their demons in the honesty of the landscape, be it alone or among a native people with a more rightly-aligned set of values. This tale has been told again and again both in literary form and contemporary film. There is some element of hope for the hopeless found in these stories that speak to the profound depths of our weariness and sparks in even the most disillusioned soul the hope of peace and a quiet life of meaning.

Since that time in the Sangre de Cristo Mountains, I no longer seek those things that help me to heal but for those things that fortify me with the strength required to carry the load fate has set upon my shoulders. Instead of finding a way to *forget*, find a way to bear the constant remembering. The silence of the wild being one of those elements that reinforce the weathered walls of the soul and mind.

There are days when life is complex and I require some answer to the how's and why's that surround the mysterious forces at work in my life. And still there are days when life is simple, and all I need is a heavy coat to wrap around me, a sturdy pair of boots, and a bag big enough to carry my load. There are those days when, emptied by the hardships to befall me, I require a great deal for happiness—those dark days when the worth of being alive eludes me in my haze of weariness. But then there are those moments when small joys bring a soothing warmth to my numb heart. Those days when my suffering recedes, the gray curtain rolls back, and the beauty of what it is to draw breath pervades—those days of gratitude, appreciation, and simplicity.

Rio Grande Gorge, Taos, New Mexico

RADICAL AUTHENTICITY

"Dad said I would always be 'high minded and low waged'
from reading too much Ralph Waldo Emerson.
Maybe he was right."
–JIM HARRISON, *The English Major*

DURING THE BOOK TOUR FOR MY CHILDREN'S novel, I was asked to forecast the next frontier of creativity. The question posed: *In a world where we are desensitized and saturated with information but little wisdom, what is a writer's place?* Around the same time, another question of a much more personal nature was likewise put in my path. It came when I told Mal that I planned to write about the C-PTSD and miscarriage. Knowing how guarded I was as a person, she asked, "Why share this with the world? Why put that much of yourself out there?"

The answer came forth from me easily and fully-formed, as though I had been silently incubating its truth for years. Oddly, it was the answer to both the questions asked of me—professional and personal alike—I replied to her, "Because I believe, the next frontier of creativity is *radical authenticity*."

You see, we are tired of being bombarded with ADs and honing social media personas. What we all seek are connection and understanding. The digital age is supposed to link us but we have never been more disconnected from ourselves and one another as we are now. Humanity is starved for connection. We see manifestations of this emptiness in our toxic lifestyles. We binge on all things, be it work, food, alcohol, shopping, digital distractions, and so on, in an effort to quell this acidic loneliness burning through us.

As a writer—an artist—I ask myself, *What's next? Where is the next boundary to push? What is the next thing of which humanity is in need that I might make some small contribution to it?* And, over the last months, I have come to believe that next revelatory action isn't one of shock-for-shock's sake such as what we see in the mainstream media, but one of humble baring, of nakedness, of vulnerability . . . of radical authenticity. So, I will stand bare within these pages, as honest as I can be. Not asking for pity. Not pretending to have answers. But simply presenting my journey in order to let others who have endured similar trauma know they are not alone.

Why share all this with the world? Why put this much of myself out there? because I'm broken. We're all broken and right now we're all isolated within that brokenness. The cure for the loneliness is connection—connection with that broken part of ourselves and with each other—and we can't achieve that connection while pretending we are okay. We're *not* okay.

My previously published works were a lotus—an expression of hope—but I knew I had yet to speak of *the mud*—the darkness which makes these manifestations of hope an achievement of *transcendence* rather than simply one of literary merit. For me, leaving the story untold wasn't an option. I would have to tell everything that had happened not only for my own process of catharsis but for what I hoped to do as an author—to help highlight how we are all moving across the same terrain and suffering the same affliction.

To those closest to me—who have witnessed my inner-turmoil—my confession of having C-PTSD will give *context*. That said, the admission of this diagnosis will come as a surprise to many of my colleagues. By most measures, I am "high-functioning." I am an award-winning independent writer, successful business owner, I sit on three different boards, I've attended rigorous universities, etc . . . I am one of those people who, to look at, appears to be well-adjusted, healthy, and successful. Not because I entirely am but, rather, because my work has been a method of dissociating myself from my trauma.

In *Trauma and Recovery*, Judith Lewis Herman writes, "The conflict between the will to deny horrible events and the will to proclaim them aloud is the central dialectic of psychological trauma." To confess that I suffer from C-PTSD, struggle with depression, and have dwelled in a mind-space wherein suicide seemed the only option left, leaves me open to the judgment of others.

I've worked for 15 years to build respect within my industry and some would argue that, by confessing such inflictions, I risk losing the ground I have gained. We all know the stigma mental illness carries with it. But I would like to think, I've spent 15 years, not honing a façade to be maintained but coming into myself, and speaking of this struggle is the next door through which I must pass. I speak of my trials to put a face to mental illness and dispel the stigma of "weakness" and to say, yes, I am broken but so are we all.

Suicide was an "option" in my mind, not because I wanted to die but because I wanted the pain to end, and, as hopeless as I was, by my own hand was the only way I could see the pain ending. That is, until I realized that killing one's self doesn't end the pain but transfers it to those closest to you. When one commits suicide, the pain doesn't get quelled when their life is extinguished but magnified and projected out onto others like shrapnel from a bomb of despair. When I came to this truth the idea of suicide, which followed me, was no longer the answer because my love for those around me was greater than any other emotion I felt or need I had. I am grateful for those around me who steadied me during this mental extreme that I lived to see the good days ahead.

There was a time when I looked back on the circumstances of my life and was certain I'd been broken by everything that had happened. As an author, I explore metaphysical and philosophical matters. During the worst of it, onlookers who have learned my story often comment to me that, "All the hardships you suffered were part of a divine plan for your life because something good came from each bad thing." As though a divine presence decided to teach me these great lessons through pain. I am affronted by such a suggestion because it robs me of my accomplishment by removing the element of transcendence.

I don't believe we learn anything from suffering. If human beings inherently learned through suffering, we would be a population of enlightened beings and we're not. We learn from suffering *if and only if* we manage to transcend our suffering to find meaning in what is otherwise senseless. This process of transcendence is a profoundly human one that imparts the deepest—most lasting—sense of achievement. Each one of my books—this essay—is an expression of my effort to transcend something senseless to befall me. The events of my life crushed me and rightfully so but I live on in the wake of it. After all that has happened, I cannot help but come to believe, there should be a disclaimer for the soul upon entering this life stating: *This will destroy you but it is not the end.* Every immortal thing must die once to learn that it is immortal. One life ends but another begins.

End Notes

1. Aktalakota.stjo.org. (2017). *Sacred Buffalo - Akta Lakota Museum & Cultural Center.* [online] Available at: http://aktalakota.stjo.org site/News2?page=NewsArticle&id=8596 [Accessed May 2017] and Bray, Kingsley M. *Crazy Horse: a Lakota life.* Norman: University of Oklahoma, 2008.

2. "Complex Post Traumatic Stress Disorder (C-PTSD)." *Out of the Fog.* November 17, 2015. Accessed May 28, 2016. http://outofthefog website/toolbox-1/2015/11/17/complex-post traumatic-stress-disorder-c-ptsd.

3. Robert Julyan, *The Place Names of New Mexico,* University of New Mexico Press, 1998.

4. Hamill, Toni; The Manitou Springs Heritage Center. *Garden of the Gods.* Charleston, SC: Arcadia Publishing., 2012.

Taos, New Mexico

About the Author

L.M. Browning is an award-winning author of twelve books. In her writing, Browning explores the confluence of the natural landscape and the interior landscape. In 2010, she debuted with a three-title contemplative poetry series. These three books went on to garner several accolades including a total of 3 pushcart-prize nominations, the Nautilus Gold Medal for Poetry, and *Foreword Reviews*' Book of the Year Award. She has freelanced for several publications and has a biannual interview column in *The Wayfarer* magazine in which she has interviewed dozens of notable creative figures such as Academy Award-Nominated filmmaker Tomm Moore, Peabody-winning host of *On Being* Krista Tippett and celebrated poet David Whyte.

Balancing her passion for writing with her love of learning, Browning is a graduate of the University of London, a Fellow with the International League of Conservation Writers and sits on the Board of the Independent Book Publishers Association. In 2011, she opened Homebound Publications. She is currently working to complete a L.B.A. in Creative Writing at Harvard University's Extension School in Cambridge, Massachusetts.

visit her at www.lmbrowning.com

LITTLE
BOUND BOOKS
SMALL BOOKS, BIG IMPACT

The Little Bound Books Essay Series
Personal. Poignant. Powerful.

WWW.HOMEBOUNDPUBLICATIONS.COM

HOMEBOUND PUBLICATIONS

Ensuring that the mainstream isn't the only stream.

At Homebound Publications we publish books written by independent voices for independent minds. Our books focus on a return to simplicity and balance, connection to the earth and each other, and the search for meaning and authenticity. Founded in 2011, Homebound Publications is one of the rising independent publishers in the country. Collectively through our imprints, we publish between fifteen to twenty offerings each year. Our authors have received dozens of awards, including: *Foreword Reviews'* Indie Awards, Nautilus Book Award, Benjamin Franklin Book Awards, and Saltire Literary Awards. Highly-respected among bookstores, readers and authors alike, Homebound Publications has a proven devotion to quality, originality and integrity.

We are a small press with big ideas. As an independent publisher we strive to ensure that the mainstream is not the only stream. It is our intention at Homebound Publications to preserve contemplative storytelling. We publish full-length introspective works of creative non-fiction as well as essay collections, travel writing, poetry, and novels. In all our titles, our intention is to introduce new perspectives that will directly aid humankind in the trials we face at present as a global village.